Nature's Cycles
Water

Dana Meachen Rau

Marshall Cavendish
Benchmark
New York

It is a rainy day!

Rain is water that falls from the sky. You can watch the rain from your window.

Water falls down to the Earth. Then it will go back up into the air. Then it will fall down again. That is the *water cycle*.

Look at a *globe*. The blue parts are water. Most of Earth is covered with water. The water is in Earth's oceans. Earth also has water in rivers and lakes. Water is a *liquid*. That means it can be poured.

8

The sun makes water *evaporate*. This means liquid water changes to *water vapor*. Water vapor is water in the air that you cannot see. *Humidity* is the amount of water vapor in the air.

Think of a wet towel by the pool. The sun's heat makes the water evaporate. Then the towel is dry. The water is now in the air as water vapor.

Water evaporates from
oceans, rivers, and lakes.
Not all the water evaporates.
A lot stays behind.

Water even evaporates from
your skin when you sweat!

14

Water vapor in the air turns
into drops of liquid water.
These drops make clouds.
Clouds get heavy with water.
The water drops to the ground.

If the *temperature* is warm, the water falls as rain.

If the temperature is cold, the water falls as snow or ice.

Most rain falls into oceans. Rain falls onto land. Rain also falls into rivers and lakes.

Rain goes into the ground.
Plants need water to live.
Their roots soak up some of
this water.

Most water travels deep underground. It soaks down into the *soil*. This water is called *groundwater*.

On land, streams flow into rivers. Rivers flow into oceans. Groundwater travels back toward the ocean, too. It flows slowly under the ground.

Water in the oceans evaporates again. Cool air turns water vapor into drops that make clouds. The clouds drop the water back to Earth.

Earth has always had the same amount of water. It gets reused over and over again. Watch the water cycle at work!

Challenge Words

evaporate (ee-VAP-uhr-ate)—To change from liquid water to water vapor.

globe—A round map of earth.

groundwater—Water traveling through soil deep underground.

humidity (hyoo-MID-i-tee)—The amount of water vapor in the air.

liquid (LIK-wid)—A substance that can be poured and that takes the shape of its container.

soil—The earth in which plants grow.

temperature (TEM-pruh-chuhr)—How hot or cold the air is.

water cycle (water SY-kuhl)—The series of things that happen over and over again as water turns to water vapor, water vapor becomes clouds, and clouds rain back down to the ground.

water vapor (water VAP-puhr)—Water in the air that you cannot see.

Index

Page numbers in **boldface** are illustrations.

The author would like to thank Paula Meachen
for her scientific guidance and expertise in reviewing this book.

With thanks to Nanci Vargus, Ed.D.,
and Beth Walker Gambro, reading consultants

Marshall Cavendish Benchmark
99 White Plains Road
Tarrytown, New York 10591-9001
www.marshallcavendish.us

Text copyright © 2010 by Marshall Cavendish Corporation

Library of Congress Cataloging-in-Publication Data

Rau, Dana Meachen, 1971–
Water / by Dana Meachen Rau.
p. cm. — (Bookworms. Nature's cycles)
Includes index.
Summary: "Introduces the idea that many things in the world around us are cyclical in nature
and discusses the water cycle from puddle to cloud to rain to puddle again"—Provided by publisher.
ISBN 978-0-7614-4099-4
1. Hydrologic cycle—Juvenile literature. I. Title.
GB848.R38 2009
551.48—dc22
2008042505

Editor: Christina Gardeski
Publisher: Michelle Bisson
Designer: Virginia Pope
Art Director: Anahid Hamparian

Photo Research by Anne Burns Images

Cover Photo by *Getty Images*/Daryl Benson

The photographs in this book are used with permission and through the courtesy of:
Corbis: pp. 1, 20 Rainman/zefa; p. 8 Bill Ross; p. 11 George Contorakes; p. 16 Mark Mawson;
p. 28 The Irish Image Collection. *Photo Edit*: p. 2 Felicia Martinez; p. 7 Michael Newman. *Photri Microstock*:
pp. 4, 24. *Photo Researchers*: p. 12 Michael Gadomski; p. 23 Nigel Cattlin. *Getty Images*: p. 13 Miroku;
p. 14 Adrian Nakic; p. 17 Marc Wilson Photography; p. 19 Stuart Westmorland. *Peter Arnold*: p. 27 Joerg Boethling.

Printed in Malaysia
1 3 5 6 4 2